A DAY IN LONDON

Les

Burke Books ▶ **LONDON ✶ TORONTO ✶ NEW YORK**

First published 1982
Reprinted 1984
© Lesley Anne Ivory 1982

ISBN 0 222 00785 0 Hardbound
ISBN 0 222 00787 7 Softback

Burke Publishing Company Limited
Pegasus House, 116–120 Golden Lane, London EC1Y 0TL, England.
Burke Publishing (Canada) Limited
Registered Office: 20 Queen Street West, Suite 3000
Box 30, Toronto, Canada M5H 1V5.
Burke Publishing Company Inc.
Registered Office: 333 State Street, PO Box 1740
Bridgeport, Connecticut 06601, U.S.A.
Printed in the Netherlands by Deltaprint Holland

London is the biggest city in England. 3

Near the centre of London
is Buckingham Palace
where the royal family live.

On special occasions
they ride in the golden state coach.

This is one of the Queen's guards.

The guards at the Tower of London
are called beefeaters.

The royal crowns and jewels
are kept safe in the Tower.

Outside there are old guns
 and some black birds called ravens. 11

London streets are very busy.

This man is a pavement artist. 13

London has lovely parks

. . . and squares.

Julie is feeding the ducks and flamingoes
in St. James's Park.

Tom is watching the monkeys' tea-party
at the London Zoo.

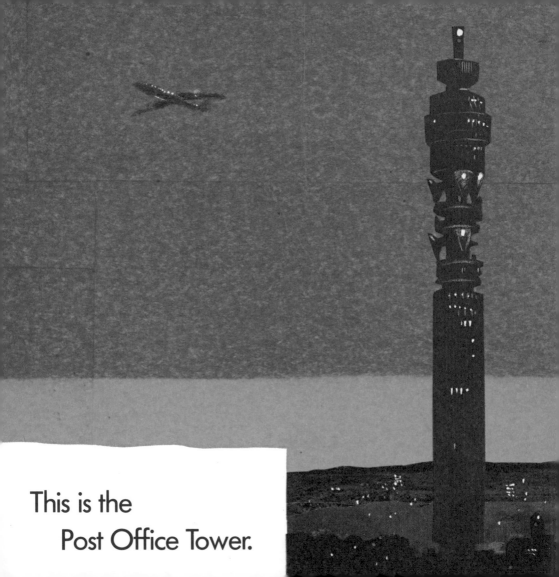

This is the
Post Office Tower.

Up there is Lord Nelson.

We are going through a tunnel
under the streets of London.

We are riding in an underground train.

These people are taking a boat trip
on the River Thames.
The boat is going under Tower Bridge.

Big Ben,
    the famous clock
    at Westminster,
    strikes tea-time.